DK SUPER Planet

Sharing the PLANET

Our amazing planet is home to a diverse variety of life—learn how we can protect and conserve it for generations to come

Produced for DK by
Editorial Just Content Limited
Design Studio Noel

Author Amanda Oberswain

Senior Editor Amelia Jones
Senior Art Editor Gilda Pacitti
Managing Editor Katherine Neep
Managing Art Editor Sarah Corcoran
Production Editor Jaypal Chauhan
DTP Designer Rohit Singh
Production Controller Rebecca Parton
Publisher Sarah Forbes
Managing Director, Learning Hilary Fine

First American Edition, 2025
Published in the United States by DK Publishing,
a division of Penguin Random House LLC
1745 Broadway, 20th Floor, New York, NY 10019

Copyright © 2025 Dorling Kindersley Limited
25 26 27 28 29 10 9 8 7 6 5 4 3 2 1
001–345525–Apr/2025

All rights reserved.
Without limiting the rights under the copyright reserved
above, no part of this publication may be reproduced, stored
in or introduced into a retrieval system, or transmitted, in any
form, or by any means (electronic, mechanical, photocopying,
recording, or otherwise), without the prior written permission
of the copyright owner.
Published in Great Britain by Dorling Kindersley Limited

A catalog record for this book
is available from the Library of Congress.
HC ISBN: 978-0-5939-6604-4
PB ISBN: 978-0-5939-6603-7

DK books are available at special discounts when purchased
in bulk for sales promotions, premiums, fund-raising,
or educational use.
For details, contact: DK Publishing Special Markets,
1745 Broadway, 20th Floor, New York, NY 10019
SpecialSales@dk.com

Printed and bound in China

www.dk.com

Contents

Our Planet Earth	4
Earth's Systems	6
Finite Resources	8
Recycling and Reusing	10
Renewable Resources	12
Sharing our Planet's Resources	14
The Importance of Nature	16
Endangered Species	18
Conservation	20
Sharing our Planet with Living Things	22
The Importance of Community	24
Relationships between Communities	26
Sharing our Planet with Each Other	28
Being Global Citizens	30
Sharing our Ideas to Help the Planet	32
Everyday Science: Rewilding	34
Everyday Science: Ocean Cleanup	36
Let's Experiment! Recycled Bookmarks	38
Let's Experiment! Crafting Containers	40
Vocabulary Builder: Community Bulletin	42
Glossary	44
Index	46

Words in **bold** are explained in the glossary on page 44.

Our
PLANET EARTH

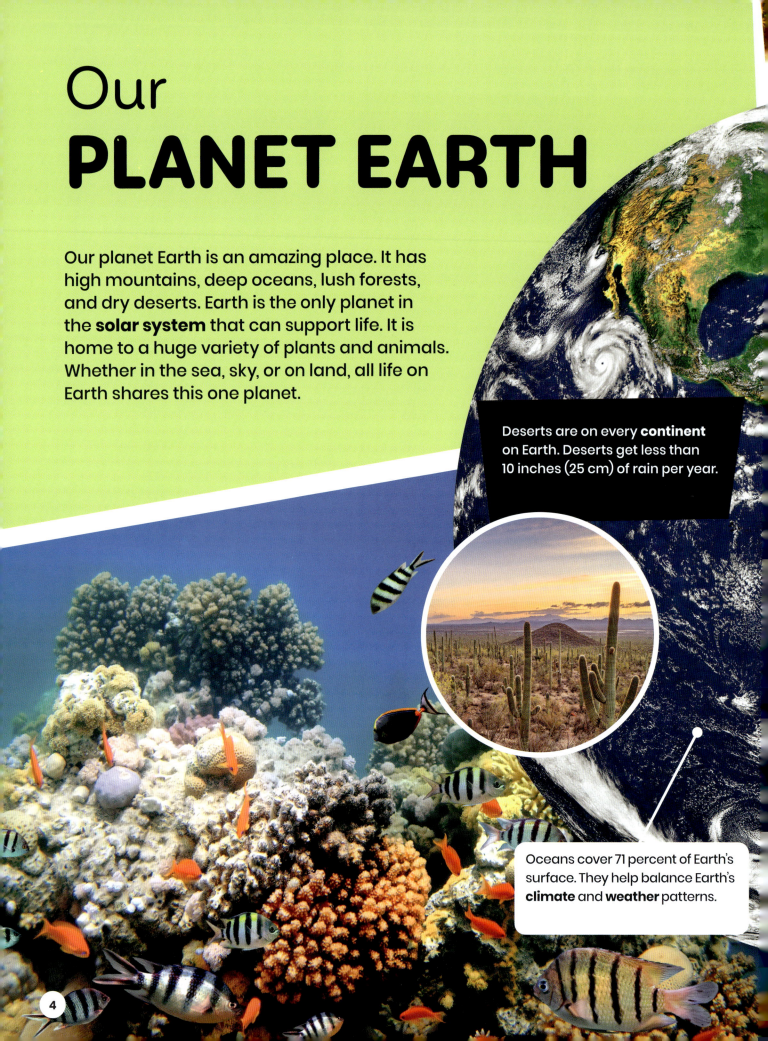

Our planet Earth is an amazing place. It has high mountains, deep oceans, lush forests, and dry deserts. Earth is the only planet in the **solar system** that can support life. It is home to a huge variety of plants and animals. Whether in the sea, sky, or on land, all life on Earth shares this one planet.

Deserts are on every **continent** on Earth. Deserts get less than 10 inches (25 cm) of rain per year.

Oceans cover 71 percent of Earth's surface. They help balance Earth's **climate** and **weather** patterns.

New York City is home to more than 8 million people. It is the biggest city in the USA.

Earth is often called the "blue planet" because of the liquid water in our oceans. From space, most of the planet looks blue.

There are **rainforests** all over Earth. The world's largest rainforest is the Amazon. It is a **tropical** rainforest.

Tundras are cold regions near Earth's poles. They can also be found on mountaintops. Tundras are so cold that trees do not grow there.

Farmers around the world use Earth's **resources** to grow food for people to eat.

Earth's SYSTEMS

Planet Earth is a **system** made up of smaller systems. Each system is linked together. Earth's four main systems are called spheres. The spheres contain all water, air, land, and life on Earth. The connections between the four spheres create the necessary conditions for life.

The **hydrosphere** contains all water on Earth: liquid water, solid ice, and water vapor. Almost all water on Earth is salt water.

Fascinating fact

The northern and southern lights (aurora borealis and aurora australis) are caused by particles from the Sun interacting with Earth's **atmosphere**.

The atmosphere contains the gases surrounding Earth. It reaches from Earth's surface to over 6,214 miles (10,000 km) into space.

The **biosphere** contains all life on Earth. Life on Earth is organized into groups called **kingdoms**. Humans are part of the animal kingdom.

The **geosphere** is the land, or solid crust, on Earth. It includes all of Earth's **landforms**, like mountains, valleys, and plains.

Finite RESOURCES

The Earth is full of resources. Resources are anything found in nature that humans can use. Many of Earth's resources are **finite**, which means there is a limited amount of them. Many finite resources are also **nonrenewable**. This means that once we use them, they are gone for good.

Fascinating fact

Fossil fuels are formed from the remains of **ancient** plants and animals. This process took millions of years.

FOSSIL FUELS

Fossil fuels are found in Earth's crust. We burn fuels to produce electricity and heat. We use them to make things like gasoline and plastic.

METALS AND MINERALS

Minerals and metals are mined from Earth's crust. They are used in many ways: in buildings, computers and **technology**, cars, jewelry, and even soda cans.

FRESH WATER

Fresh water is a finite resource that is **renewable**. Only 3 percent of Earth's water is fresh water. We use fresh water for drinking and growing crops.

Recycling and REUSING

Many of Earth's finite resources can be recycled and reused. Reusing means using a thing again, like taking cloth bags to the grocery store instead of using disposable plastic ones. **Recycling** is a process that turns used resources into updated ones. This allows the resources to be used again in new ways. It helps stop them from running out.

Used paper can be turned into recycled paper and paper goods. Making and using recycled paper saves energy and trees.

Some plastic can be recycled into clothes! These fleece tops are made from recycled plastic bottles.

Glass and aluminum can be recycled again and again. These materials can be reformed to make new cans and jars.

People can donate and reuse clothes at vintage stores or thrift shops. Buying secondhand clothes saves energy and reduces waste.

HOW PAPER IS RECYCLED

1 Used paper is shredded and turned into pulp.

2 Paper pulp is recolored and dried.

3 The pulp is pressed and rolled together. It then moves through heated rollers.

4 The paper is smoothed through more rollers. It is ready to use!

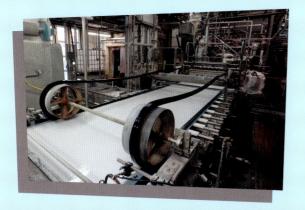

Renewable RESOURCES

Some of Earth's resources are **renewable**. Nature can replace renewable resources fast enough for humans to reuse them easily. Finite resources can run out, but there are lots of renewable resources. Renewable resources can power our homes, cities, and even our futures. Scientists and engineers are making technologies powered by renewable resources.

This tower in Spain collects sunlight using lots of big mirrors. When the sunlight hits the top of the tower, it heats up water to create **steam**. This steam is used turn a big wheel called a **turbine**, which makes electricity.

SOLAR POWER
Solar power is energy from the Sun.

Solar cells take in the Sun's energy. They turn it into electricity. Solar cells only work during the day.

Find out!

Can you find out what renewable energy resources there are where you live?

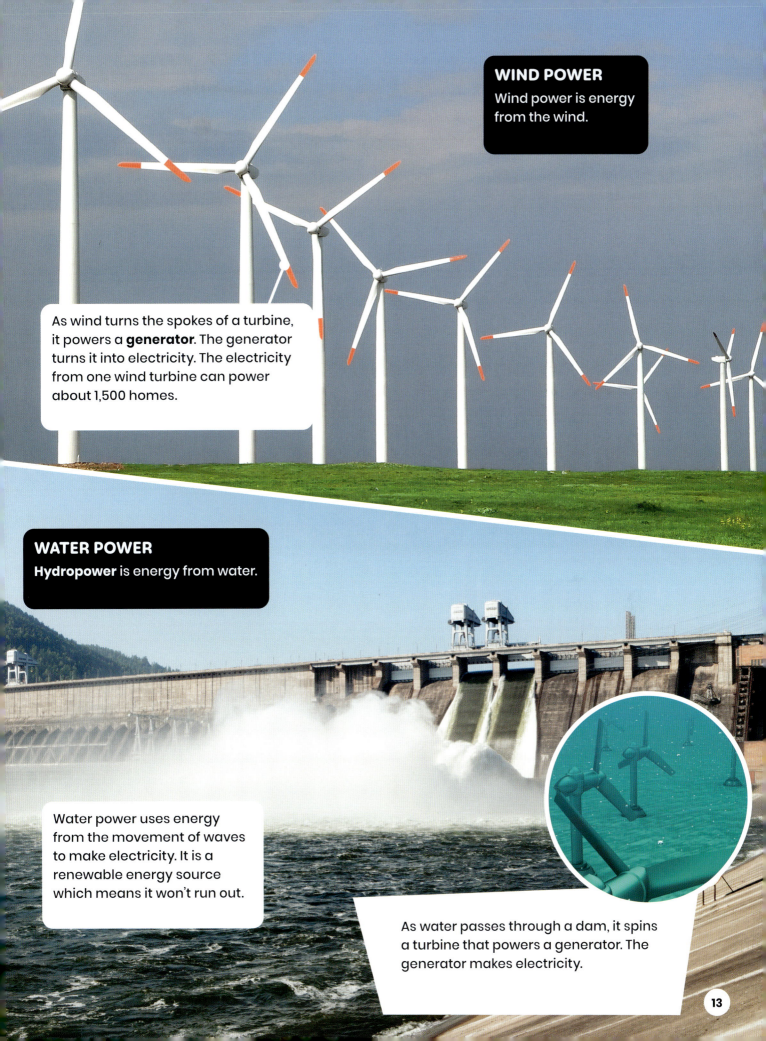

WIND POWER
Wind power is energy from the wind.

As wind turns the spokes of a turbine, it powers a **generator**. The generator turns it into electricity. The electricity from one wind turbine can power about 1,500 homes.

WATER POWER
Hydropower is energy from water.

Water power uses energy from the movement of waves to make electricity. It is a renewable energy source which means it won't run out.

As water passes through a dam, it spins a turbine that powers a generator. The generator makes electricity.

Sharing our Planet's RESOURCES

More than 8 billion people live on Earth. We all need resources like food, water, shelter, and clean air to live. We use other resources, like metals and minerals, to improve our lives. Some of these resources are nonrenewable. This is why we all need to share Earth's resources—to make sure there is enoughfor everyone.

METALS AND MINERALS
These resources are finite and nonrenewable. Many can be recycled and reused.

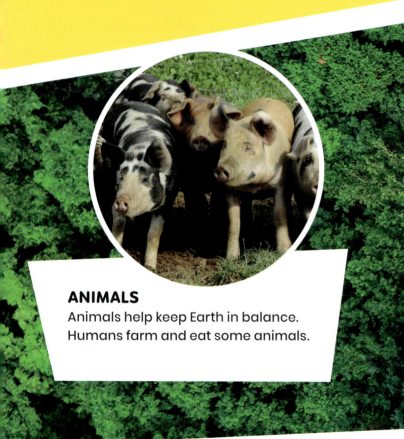

ANIMALS
Animals help keep Earth in balance. Humans farm and eat some animals.

FORESTS
Forests give us clean air to breathe and materials for shelter. Forests can be found on almost every continent.

FOSSIL FUELS
Like metals and minerals, resources are finite and nonrenewable. They will run out at some point in time. Scientists and engineers are developing renewable alternatives.

AIR
Clean air is a human need. Wind can be used to make electricity.

WATER
Access to clean, fresh water is a human need. Water can be used to produce electricity.

SUN
The Sun provides energy for all living things on Earth. Solar power can be used to make electricity.

SOIL
Soil is essential for growing plants that provide food for both people and **livestock**.

The Importance of NATURE

Life on Earth exists in all shapes, sizes, and colors. Scientists estimate there are over 8 million **species** on the planet, with millions more yet to be discovered. Earth's rich **biodiversity** keeps our planet in balance. The variety of living things, including plants and animals, is what makes Earth home.

OCEANS
Most humpback whales live in the Pacific Ocean.

TUNDRA
Flowers grow in dry, rocky areas of the Arctic.

Tree frogs thrive in the Amazon rainforest.

Polar bears live in the Arctic tundra.

RAINFORESTS
Lemurs live in the rainforest in Madagascar.

FRESHWATER
Lily pads grow on lake surfaces in Florida.

Elephants are at home in the Kenyan **savannas**.

Carp thrive in the St. Lawrence River in North America.

Seagrass grows in the Mediterranean Sea.

GRASSLANDS
Many kangaroos live in the grasslands of Australia.

BOREAL FOREST
The boreal forest, also known as the taiga, is a very large forest found in northern regions. It is home to various wildlife, including brown bears.

Horned vipers are native to the Sahara Desert.

Pine trees are common in the forests of Norway.

DESERTS
Prickly pear cactus plants grow well in the deserts of the Americas.

Endangered SPECIES

All species on Earth are connected. When life on Earth is not in balance, species can become **endangered**. Endangered species have low populations. They are at risk of going **extinct**. A species goes extinct when there are no more living members. Pollution, **habitat** loss, and climate change are some human-caused risks that endanger some species.

Fascinating fact

Migrating sea turtles travel up to 10,000 miles (16,000 km) every year.

There are seven species of sea turtles on Earth. Most of them are endangered. Humans are the biggest threat to sea turtles.

Sea turtles travel great distances across Earth's oceans to lay their eggs on land. Habitat loss and shore destruction harm the sea turtle population.

Fishing gear and nets accidentally catch over 250,000 sea turtles each year.

Rising ocean temperatures cause changes in **ocean currents**. This can decrease the food available to sea turtles. Storms caused by climate change can destroy their habitats.

Pollution caused by humans injures and kills thousands of turtles each year. It can take hundreds of years or more for plastic to break down in the ocean.

CONSERVATION

It is up to us to protect Earth's species and keep Earth in balance. One way we can do this is by practicing **conservation**. Conservation means preserving and protecting Earth's resources. This includes plants and animals. Conservation efforts are in place for many endangered species on Earth.

Scientists can monitor animals by tracking their movements and behavior using radio tag collars.

Conservationists dig up sea turtle nests to see if the eggs hatched.

Scientists collect data on turtle **migration** patterns. Conservation groups use this data to stop **fisheries** from going into turtle areas.

Some shorelines are used as conservation zones for sea turtles. This guards them from human development so turtles can safely lay their eggs.

Using reusable bags and bottles can help keep plastic pollution out of the ocean. One plastic water bottle can remain in the ocean for 450 years.

Keeping the ocean clean and free of fishing equipment helps protect sea turtles.

Sharing our Planet with LIVING THINGS

Bees are essential for human survival. But bee numbers have decreased over the past 100 years. This is due to habitat destruction and other human environmental impacts. We can help boost bee populations through conservation efforts. Two ways are beekeeping and planting wildflowers. This provides habitats for bees to survive and grow.

Fascinating fact

Not all bees live in colonies. Some bees, like the mason bee, live alone.

Bees are a **keystone species**. This means they are essential for the survival of other species.

Every time a bee visits a flower for food, they transfer pollen in a process called **pollination**. Pollination creates more flowers, fruits, and seeds for new plants.

Honeybees live in large **communities** called colonies. Bee colonies can include up to 50,000 bees.

Honeybees turn the nectar they collect from flowers into honey. Honey varies in color and taste based on the nectar used.

The Importance of COMMUNITY

A community is a diverse group of people with something in common. Members of a community might share similar locations, interests, values, or goals. You can be part of many different communities. Examples of communities are schools, towns, and even global online communities. We rely on and support each other through community.

People in communities work together to help make their environment a better place. This person is removing trash from the beach.

People can look after public areas, keeping them clean. Neighbors can share food or lend tools or toys to other families. People can volunteer to fix things. They can share their skills and coach sports teams. Neighbors can care for sick or older people. Or they can work together to keep the area safe.

YOUR CLASSROOM

Find out!

What communities are you part of? What people are important in those communities?

YOUR SCHOOL

YOUR NEIGHBORHOOD

YOUR LOCAL AREA

Relationships between COMMUNITIES

Communities help each other solve problems. Some problems need communities to work together around the world. Smaller communities can handle local issues, like a school and its neighborhood. For example, communities can work on big problems like climate change, or fix local issues like making bike lanes safer. When we work together, we make things better for ourselves and the planet.

The UN has 17 goals to make the world a better place for people and our planet by the year 2030. They are called the UN Sustainable Development Goals. They include things like making sure everyone has enough to eat, making sure all children can to go to school, and keeping the planet clean.

The United Nations (UN) is a worldwide community of nations. It works to find solutions for global issues.

Fascinating fact

The UN has 193 member countries.

School communities and their local areas overlap in many ways. They work together to support each other.

Urban communities are more densely **populated** than **rural** communities. This means that more people live there.

This floating market in Thailand provides fresh food for the local community.

Sharing our Planet
WITH EACH OTHER

North Africa is one of the hottest, driest regions on Earth. As temperatures around the world increase due to climate change, nations across Africa are working together to build a "Great Green Wall." This wall will be made of trees. It will increase plant and animal life in the region.

Fascinating fact

Once it is completed, the Great Green Wall is likely to become a new world wonder.

The Great Green Wall is creating jobs for people across Africa. These women are planting trees. As the trees grow, they will provide habitats for wildlife.

The landscape in the region is very dry and **arid**. There are few habitats for plants and animals.

Communities are planting trees, like the acacia tree, that can survive in the hot desert climate. They add nutrients back to the soil.

Africa

The Great Green Wall will stretch east to west across 22 different countries. That is around 5,000 miles (8,000 km).

The trees in the Great Green Wall will remove over 275 million tons (250 million metric tons) of **greenhouse gases** from Earth's atmosphere, reducing the impacts of climate change.

Being Global CITIZENS

As **citizens** of Earth, we all have a duty to take care of Earth and each other. We must look after Earth's health, future, resources, and living things. The Olympic Games are one way for global citizens to meet. They allow us to share ideas, compete, and spread unity around the globe. The Olympics are a celebration of humanity.

The five Olympic rings symbolize peace, unity, and friendship between nations. The flame represents our connection to the past as we move into the future.

Find out!

What are other ways you can be a global citizen?

The Olympics open with a Parade of Nations. This includes music, dancing, and performances. Athletes wear colors and costumes that represent their nation.

Athletes race in the men's 100m final in the 2024 Summer Olympics in Paris, France.

Athletes compete in wheelchair racing in the 2012 Summer Paralympics in London, UK.

A skier from Austria competes in the 2024 Winter Youth Olympics in Gangwon, South Korea.

Athletes race at the 2024 Summer Olympics in Paris, France.

BE A GLOBAL CITIZEN

You can be a good global citizen too. Work toward equality. Make green choices to protect Earth. Stand up for others.

Simone Biles is an American Olympic gymnast. She has won gold medals and inspired people around the world.

31

Sharing our Ideas to HELP THE PLANET

Every living thing on Earth has the right to a safe, healthy planet. We can use our voices to protect the planet, its resources, and all the plants and animals that live here. Kids have voices, too. Use your voice to share ideas and speak up for our planet.

Climate marches are ways to get involved and demand climate action. Climate action can protect the future of the planet.

Find out!

How can you use your voice to speak up for the planet?

Talking with your family and community is one way to share ideas and look after the planet.

Write letters or speak to elected officials to demand climate action. Laws passed to look after Earth's resources will keep the planet in balance today and in the future.

Planting a tree is a great way to get involved. Trees provide clean air for us to breathe and shade to protect against rising temperatures.

Everyday SCIENCE
Rewilding

You can support Earth in your backyard. **Native plants** provide food and habitats for many important animals, like pollinators. People around the world are adding native plants to their lawns, rooftops, windows, and balconies. This can protect biodiversity and support Earth.

This public garden in Arizona contains native plants that do not need additional fertilizer and water to thrive.

Gardens can grow food for people and animals. Some gardens are full of flowers. Even vegetable and fruit gardens produce flowers as they grow.

In the fall, do not rake up fallen leaves. Leaving them on the ground provides food and habitats for wildlife through the winter.

Turn part of your lawn into a wild garden. Add wildflowers and other native plants. Weeds like milkweed feed caterpillars and monarch butterflies.

Many cities add green spaces to support wildlife and fight climate change. Trees and plants help clean the air we breathe. They provide shade to keep cities cool.

Some communities let their yards grow for the whole month of May. Long grasses and flowers provide food for pollinators like bees.

People who live in apartment buildings can add plants to their windows or balconies to help protect the planet.

Rewilding near you

Rewilding where we live helps the plants and animals that live in our area. How do you think plants and animals in your area might use these spaces?

Everyday SCIENCE
Ocean Cleanup

More than 1.2 million tons (1.15 million metric tons) of plastic enter the ocean each year. This huge amount of garbage threatens Earth's marine life. And the effects are reaching land. Scientists and engineers are working on new ocean cleanup technology to remove the plastic and reverse the damage.

The Great Pacific Garbage Patch is an island of trash in the Pacific Ocean. It is approximately 620,000 sq miles (1.6 million sq km).

Most plastic in oceans comes from plastic pollution in rivers. The Interceptor is a boat that cleans up rivers. There are 15 Interceptors in eight countries around the world.

There is more trash in the dark red parts of the patch.

Most of the trash in the Great Pacific Garbage Patch is plastic.

Ocean cleanups are a great way to help remove waste and keep our beaches clean.

Once it is collected, some plastic can be recycled and reused.

Let's EXPERIMENT!

RECYCLED BOOKMARKS

There are lots of fun ways to reduce waste and be creative! In this experiment, you will make your own recycled bookmarks.

You will need:
- Ripped-up pieces of scrap paper
- A bowl
- Warm water
- A dish towel
- A tray
- A sponge
- Scissors
- Decorations, including ribbons

1 Put the scrap paper in a bowl. Add warm water. Let the mixture soak for about an hour.

Be careful when cutting the bookmark shapes. You can ask an adult to help you.

2 Squeeze the water out of the paper mixture (pulp) with your hands.

3 Place a dish towel on a tray. Add a layer of the pulp on top of the dish towel. Then, fold the rest of the towel over the top.

4 Use a sponge to soak up the moisture. Leave the pulp to dry for two days. Then, carefully lift it out of the tray.

5 Cut bookmark shapes out of the dried pulp. Decorate your bookmarks!

A PAPER MILL

It takes a lot of trees to make paper. By reusing paper, you can have fun making something new and help the environment. If you can't reuse it, remember that recycling just 1 ton of paper can help save 17 mature trees. And that saves enough energy to power an average home for up to six months!

Let's EXPERIMENT!

CRAFTING CONTAINERS

You do not have to throw plastic cups away. Instead, use them to make containers for your pens and anything else you can think of!

You will need:
- A plastic cup
- A ruler
- A permanent marker
- Scissors
- Different colors of string (fabric or plastic)
- Glue

1 Use the permanent marker and a ruler to draw evenly spaced lines around a plastic cup.

Be careful when cutting the plastic cup and the string. You can ask an adult to help you.

2 Cut along the lines you have drawn. You should leave about 0.2 inches (half a centimeter) of plastic uncut at the base of the cup.

3 Tie a knot at the end of the string. Put the knot inside the cup and place the string between two pieces of plastic.

4 Weave the string through the sections of the cup. Thread the string in front of a strip. Then, thread the string behind the next strip. Repeat this until you reach the top of the cup. Then, tie a knot in the string and cut off any extra.

5 Cut three pieces of string, and use them to make two braids to decorate. Glue one braid to the top of the container. Glue the other braid to the bottom. Your container is ready!

PLASTIC WASTE CAUSES POLLUTION

Plastic takes a long time to break down. The plastic we throw away today may still be here long after we are gone. We can reduce waste by recycling. But reusing is even better, because it keeps plastic out of the environment and saves resources.

Vocabulary BUILDER
Community Bulletin

Communities can work together to look after the planet and each other. There are lots of activities that can make a positive difference, and it is fun to work with friends and family. For example, organizing a community cleanup day is a great way to look after local parks or streets while spending time together.

Read this extract from a community bulletin below to find out about two example projects.

> We are so excited to share that our school is starting a neighborhood garden! It will grow food resources and support biodiversity in our community. Our garden will have native plants to attract wildlife species like bees. In school, we read about how some bee species are endangered. We will use this garden as a conservation area. It will help to protect bees from going extinct.
>
> But that is not all. Our families are also organizing a recycling drive to help raise money for our local food bank, which provides food for families in need. We encourage everyone to bring your recyclable materials to help with the drive. Together, we can turn trash into something new and support our food bank and the environment.

Wildlife animals, bud, compost, cuttings, fertilizer, flowers, grow, habitat, insects, leaf, mulch, nutrients, plant, pollen, protect, roots, seedling, shade, soil, stem, sunlight, water

Community assist, care, charity, donate, friendship, fundraise, gather, gift, help, improve, kindness, organize, reuse, sell, share, support, volunteer

A community garden is a great way to help care for the environment.

Recycling clothes stops them from going to waste and can help raise money for good causes.

Imagine you are writing a bulletin about a community project you took part in.

- What did you do?
- Why did you do it?

Use the words in the vocabulary box above, the example on page 42, and the prompts to help you.

Glossary

Ancient Something from a long time ago.

Atmosphere One of Earth's four main systems, made up of all the gases that surround Earth.

Arid Very dry, with little to no rainfall.

Biodiversity The variety of living things in a habitat or ecosystem.

Biosphere One of Earth's four main systems, made up of all living things on Earth

Citizen Someone who lives in a place, such as a country.

Climate The average, long-term weather conditions of a place over a period of time.

Community A group of people who have things in common.

Conservation Preserving and protecting Earth's natural resources, especially plant and animal species.

Continent One of the seven great landmasses on Earth.

Endangered Used to describe a species that is at risk of going extinct.

Extinct Used to describe a species with no more living members.

Finite Available in limited quantities.

Fishery A business that catches, processes, and sells fish and seafood.

Fossil fuels Fuels found deep in Earth's crust that are made from ancient plants and animals.

Generator A machine that turns energy into electricity.

Geosphere One of Earth's four main systems, made up of all rocks on Earth.

Greenhouse gas A gas in Earth's atmosphere that traps heat and contributes to climate change.

Habitat An environment where plants, animals, and other organisms live.

Hydropower Energy that comes from moving water.

Hydrosphere One of Earth's four main systems, made up of all water on Earth.

Keystone species A species that other species in an ecosystem depend on to survive.

Kingdom One of the five groups that all living things on Earth are divided into, including the plant kingdom and the animal kingdom.

Landform A natural feature on Earth's surface that is part of the land.

Livestock Animals that are bred and used for food and profit.

Migration A long journey to a new home.

Minerals Solid substances formed naturally in Earth's crust.

Native plants Local plants that grow in and adapt to a particular region.

Nonrenewable Used to describe something that can't grow back or refill itself once it is used.

Ocean current A movement of seawater that goes from one place to another.

Pollination The process of moving pollen from one part of a flower to another so the plant can reproduce, often carried out by insects.

Pollution Releasing harmful things into the environment.

Populated Lived in.

Rainforest A forest found in the tropical or temperate zones that is characterized by high humidity and high rainfall.

Recycling A process in which used resources are turned into updated ones.

Renewable Something, such as a natural resource, that can be replaced.

Resource Anything found on Earth that can be used by humans.

Rural The opposite of urban: the countryside, where there are no towns and fewer people live.

Savanna A type of grassland found in the tropical zone.

Solar power Energy captured from the Sun.

Solar system A group of planets and bodies that move around the Sun.

Species A group of living things that can reproduce with each other.

Steam Water vapor.

System A group of things that work together as one.

Technology Devices, systems, and methods that are created with scientific knowledge in order to help humans.

Tropical One of the world's climate zones, found near the equator.

Turbine A machine that transforms movement into energy.

Urban An area where a lot of people live and work together, like a town.

Weather The temperature and other conditions, such as rain, wind, and pressure, of a place at a particular time.

Index

A
acacia trees 29
Africa, Great Green Wall 28–29
air 15, 33
aluminum 10
Amazon rainforest 16
animals 7, 8, 14, 16–17
    see also sea turtles
Arizona 34
atmosphere 6, 7

B
bees 22–23
Biles, Simone 31
biodiversity 16, 34
biosphere 7
bookmarks, making 38–39
boreal forest 17
brown bears 17
bulletins, community 42–43

C
carp 17
citizens, global 30–31
cleanup, ocean 36–37
climate action 32–33
climate change
    and climate marches 32–33
    and the Great Green Wall 29
    and sea turtles 19
clothes, reusing 11
communities 24–25
    community bulletins 42–43
    relationships between 26–27
conservation 20–21, 22
crafting containers 40–41

D
deserts 4, 17, 29

E
Earth 4–5
    helping the planet 32–33
    resources 8–9
    systems 6–7
electricity 8, 12, 13, 15
elephants 17
endangered species 18–19
experiments 38–41
extinction 18

F
farming 5, 14, 15
fishing/fish 17, 19, 21
floating markets 27
Florida (USA) 17
forests 14, 17
fossil fuels 8, 15

G
Gangwon (South Korea) 31
gardens 34, 35
geosphere 7
glass 10
grasslands 17
Great Green Wall 28–29
Great Pacific Garbage Patch 36–37
greenhouse gases 29

H
habitats
    bees 22–23
    and rewilding 34–35
    sea turtles 19
helping the planet 32–33
honeybees 23
horned vipers 17
humpback whales 16
hydropower 13
hydrosphere 6

I
Interceptor 36

K
keystone species 23
kingdoms 7

L
lemurs 16
lily pads 17
London (UK) 31

M
Madagascar 16
metals 9, 10, 14
migration 18, 21
minerals 9, 14

N
nature 16–17
neighbors 24–25
New York City (USA) 5
northern and southern lights 6
Norway 17

O
oceans 4, 5, 16
    cleanup 36–37
    currents 19
    see also water
Olympic Games 30–31

P
paper, recycling 10–11
paper mills 39
Paris (France) 31
pine trees 17
plants 8, 16–17, 20
    and the Great Green Wall 28–29
    rewilding 34–35
plastic
    and fossil fuels 8
    pollution 19, 21, 36–37, 41
    recycling 10
polar bears 16
pollination 23
pollution, plastic 19, 21, 36–37, 41
prickly pear cactus 17

R
radio tag collars 20
rainforests 5, 16
recycling 10–11, 37
resources 5, 8–9
    renewable 12–13
    sharing 14–15
reusing 10–11, 37, 41
rewilding 34–35

S
Sahara Desert 17
St. Lawrence River 17
school communities 25, 27
sea turtles 18–19
    conservation 20–21
soil 15
solar power 12, 15
southern and northern lights 6
Spain 12
species 16
    endangered 18–19
    keystone 23
spheres 6–7
Sun 12, 15
systems 6–7

T
Thailand, floating market 27
tree frogs 16
trees 17, 28–29, 33, 39
tundras 5, 16
turbines 12, 13

U
United Nations (UN) 26
urban communities 27, 35

W
water 6, 9, 15, 17
water power 13
wave power 13
wind power 13

Acknowledgments

The publisher would like to thank the following for their kind permission to reproduce their photographs:

(Key: a-above; b-below/bottom; c-center; f-far; l-left; r-right; t-top)

123RF.com: 25bl, ANDREA 17c, Nataliia Kravchuk 7tr, navintar 8br, Dmytro Nikitin 9t, smileus 15br; **Adobe Stock**: Dimitrios 37tl, Susan Hodgson 34br, Mulderphoto 11br, Perytskyy 23cla, RLS Photo 17tc; Alamy Stock Photo: AP Photo / Leo Correa 29tl, Andrey Armyagov 21r, Associated Press / Luca Bruno 21tl, Biosphoto / Daniel Heuclin 29cra, Janice and Nolan Braud 17br, Nigel Cattlin 23cr, Cavan Images 18, Cavan Images / Christophe Launay 37cra, Cavan Images / CI2 21clb, Citizen of the Planet / Peter Bennett 43cl, Bob Daemmrich 33bl, dpa picture alliance / Frank Neuendorf 11bl, Enigma 15tr, imageBROKER / Jurgen & Christine Sohns 17cra, Eric Lafforgue 29br, Maskot 43cr, McPhoto / Lovell 34cra, Minden Pictures / Cyril Ruoso 16bc, NASA / Lee Dalton 4-5c, Brian Overcast 18-19tc, Doug Perrine 16cra, Science History Images 36tr, Enrique Shore 26b, Amy Sinns 17tl, inga spence 25br, Daniel Steeves 5b, Sam Stephenson 24cra, Charles Stirling 10b, Mel Stoutsenberger 25tr, Mary H. Swift 20tr, Emanuel Tanjala 35tl, US Navy Photo 21bl, Nathan and Elaine Vaessen 19t, Mirko Vitali 37clb, VWPics / David Salvatori 19b, Andrew Warburton 20, Libby Welch 10clb, Jeffrey Wickett 34clb, Xinhua / Mohamed Babiker 28cb; **Dreamstime.com**: 44Photography 36b, Agenturfotografin 35crb, Kouassi Gilbert Ambeu 15cr, Anankkml 15tc, Andreykuzmin 9br, Yuri Arcurs 33t, Aurovenkatesh 33br, Ocskay Bence / Obencem 7br, ChalkPhoto 6crb, Sophia Granchinho 16c, Christopher Heil 17b, Helinloik 35cl, Melanie Hobson 15bl, Hunterbliss 11crb, Vlad Ispas 41br, Francesc Xavier Bosch Janer 22-23, Jakub Krechowicz 26crb, Lornet 27cl, Marazem 10cra, Dimitar Marinov / Oorka 12t, Maryswift 21cla, Dmitri Melnik / Kinlem 14cr, Alexandr Mitiuc 13br, Monkey Business Images 24b, Fabien Monteil 18-19bc, Katie Nesling 11t, Nancy Pauwels 16-17bc, Pojoslaw 32, Seadam 17-18tc, Smandy 16br, _t_pn Kpl / Stepankapl 12b, Stanislav Tiplyashin / Siberia 13b, Sergey Uryadnikov 7cl, Wavebreakmedia Ltd 25tl, Peter Wollinga 8b, Yasushitanikado 5clb; **Getty Images**: Irina Gundareva / 500px 14br, AFP / Adrian Dennis 31cla, AFP / Franck Fife 30tr, Roy Goldsberry 9b, Richard Heathcote 31tl, Houston Chronicle / Hearst Newspapers / Smiley N. Pool 30b, john finney photography 34b, Christian Petersen 31bl, Sportsfile / Eóin Noonan 31clb, VOIGT / Tom Weller 31r; **Getty Images / iStock**: benedek 4cb, gustavofrazao 5cr, Joesboy 23tr, mbbirdy 5t, Alexey_Seafarer 16bl, SolStock 37br, vlad61 4b; **Shutterstock.com**: Connect Images - Curated 11clb, Me dia 14-15, Right Perspective Images 12tr, Visual Storyteller 27b

Cover images: *Front*: **Alamy Stock Photo**: Randy Duchaine br; **Shutterstock.com**: HutagalungArt t, Malchevska clb, STEKLO cr; *Back*: **Dreamstime.com**: Pojoslaw tl, Sergey Uryadnikov cl; **Getty Images / iStock**: vlad61 bl